Arsenic

58 Distressed Sonnets

Other books by Emily Isaacson:

Little Bird's Song

Voetelle

The Fleur-de-lis

Hours From A Convent

Ignatia

House of Rain

Snowflake Princess

A Familiar Shore

City of Roses

Victoriana

The Blossom Jar

Hallmark

Arsenic

58 Distressed Sonnets

Emily Isaacson

Potter's House Press
Canada

Cover design and interior layout: Voetelle Art & Design
Cover image: vintage Mercury sedan 1939
taken by Emily Isaacson.

ISBN: *978-1-329-34051-0*

First Edition printed 2018

Potter's House Press
Poetry Series

 Potter's House Press

is an imprint of The Wild Lily Institute
P.O. Box 3366
Mission, B.C.
Canada V2V 4J5
www.wildlilyinstitute.com

Dedicated to Grasshopper

Contents

Section I: The Early Sonnets

O beeswax, melting hotly in a glass,
we take your lit candle to the dark past . . .

—Emily Isaacson

I cannot work but linger in the field,
thus cannot eat, but walk upon the hills,
he is the facet of my trumpet pealed,
his labour drives the water from its fill.
O mortal wound, upon this silent hour;
I cannot slay me, I am overcome,
the thirst be quenched and speaking of its pow'r
in chivalry where only I am won.
He works, he toils, he sweats beneath the sun,
and I will write what nature has begun,
epiphany in me dwells to be sung—
for I am lonely, misfit, barren one.
What of my woeful rights do I procure,
to stand and now demand my life mature?

The beauty of the night aches in my core,
the lights of cities far away, now parched;
I've riveted my kingdoms, 'tis no chore,
and through the woodlands I have stately marched.
In every landscape that I've travelled by,
I've seen the sought divine touch earthly realm;
when all the other cause would question why,
I've simply stated, God is at the helm.
The hanging of the bell is one now rung,
the golden tree bequeaths the ginger pear,
I've sought to finish what I have begun
and tempered every anxious thought with care.
What reason would I capture with a lens,
when all that in its season could offend.

Winter's existence, here bow to Renoir,
tarry upon the hills with blanket white,
be the stillness of a new bride's boudoir,
the lingering of dusty snow's quiet,
with abandon I walk the silver's crust,
my dark head, with jeweled tiara, crowned,
carefree to know success in all I must—
bright silk and satin of the stately gowned,
as shoots of green appear to deck with hues
from sun on high, the newborn spring in pink
of every colour, scent; and shade of blue—
the light here dances at the meadow's brink.
The kindness of season's love maternal,
and trading for all that is eternal.

The dream is in my breast that rankled heart,
dividing soul from mind, I tore the shame
from my colourful dress, I wore the part—
singing at first light, that his holy name
were enough to make you steadfast, hungry
for more of the spirit's tell movement, light
over the wild hills and valleys, lonely
without a God that speaks in darkness, bright
as the stars, sacrifice of silver youth,
I was sitting on the park bench, lithe, soon
watching the day go by as a sun-smooth
dance: rehearsed, choreographed classic tune.
I am never more lovely than afraid,
the hopeful hand of violets in a maid.

The silver bird that eats the apples, red,
perches on the boughs, sings loud, bright and gay,
I woke and listened to his call from bed—
revived my spirit where my body lay.
Never have I heard such joyous song laud:
the simple worship of a creature, bare
to his redemption heaven would applaud,
and reap the bettering of life with care.
In each new day, the rich scent of the pines,
the forest brook which bubbles, frothy, cold—
attempt to give my soul all that is mine,
and retell in myth all I have been told.
I stretch my hands out from my infirm room
where I knew only bleak estate of doom.

The seven swans swam round the navy pond,
all there resting in white apparel, pale
in shadows, ivory as snow beyond
the emerald mountain, and meadow vale
bedecked with every lace flow'r, every hue—
their feathers fluttered lightly and coldly
in falling orange, magenta, sunset new
for one more evening, while the lead boldly
flew up and into the beauty of day
over and becoming night, the darkness
rested on the swans that swam in starkness,
lavishing the ground beneath which I lay
with spray of petals from every nation
wishing me farewell upon my station.

The immortal being, watching death come
as each proud white flower browns, falls, and dies.
The light of each soul, therein proudly won
to walk with you, hand in hand without lies
that would obscure the spirit world, longing
for that requisite touch, no man's reason—
the true quest of anyone, belonging
to the source of their power, the season
of love, of purity's wait in a line
of witnesses, choosing to be most yours;
taking you by the hand, a diamond fine
as the mortal dust rings clear from the floors.
In my heart of gold is the burning fire,
lest I should now succumb to bold desire.

Dance onward to the rhythm of my drum,
stand burnished in the bronze sunlight of day,
let the shadows sweep your soul by the way
of the iris and star it has come from;
jump at the chance to move to purplish lore,
as a magician would saw you in half,
as the mane of a horse flies by the staff,
come back from the brink of what made you poor.
Stand, hands above, and hail the royalty
we come to this place assuming to meet,
we wait, standing for hours, shifting our feet—
stare at the voice, it commands loyalty:
lilting as the sunlight on the feathers
of great birds, flying into the weather.

Do not in stagnant water flow, but swim
in the river with clear springs—at the brim
of sunlight's last clean sweep of sky, as lone
as the moons of Saturn, hung one by one
in your Creator hands, turn brevity
to song and valour emanates from this:
that the mind is theologically
inclined to do war and battles forthwith.
Take out one's sword, and triumph!—slay the foe
at this last hour, when earth is falling low;
into a field, death's horse now circles round
and ends the rider's life on gravestone mound.
What richness would this world to all direct,
that in its bosom, neither could protect.

The gardens of the night, now shadowed, still
bequeath the fragrant eve's perfume with eyes
that roam beneath the vast celestial skies
and give the notion of sequestered will.
The covered head that bows before in prayer
speaks the vows of enclosure, chastity:
rays of truth, poverty's posterity
and flowers, closed against the night's cool air.
The fountain of innumerable lights
flickering in colours, indigo, rose,
wet mist dripping off the end of my nose,
the poise of every dancing spirit, bright.
The moments of the sunken garden's verse
allure the crowds so fond of sainted earth.

The fine art of wicks, taught by yesteryear:
beeswax, in the fine golden dark honey
that melts in a puddle of riches here,
tasted first when young and without money.
Steeping tea to pour, peppermint gathers—
tasted first without white cream or sugar,
seeing if we love herbs and hot water,
speaking in a dialect of father.
O beeswax, melting hotly in a glass,
we take your lit candle to the dark past,
seeing how we are justified by love
and melting at the sight of heav'n above.
Bewitched by which is evil we succumb,
and needing of the light we come undone.

While standing against the dark, I am strong,
vigilant and overt, not succumbing
to fleeting whims of others in the wrong;
blue as the bloom of petals, bright being
translucent with the arm of paradise
at my back, a mighty army, armour
shod, a silver multitude without vice,
moving ever forward, no less vigour
in their bones than the day they first set out
to capture the castle of my heart strings,
and from the music of my soul will shout,
I am no more about the little things—
Virulent as warm honey at midday,
I taste the good of life here while it stay.

The rose immortal lends its faint perfume
to petals, mortal red upon the dawn,
and stirring of my heart, I pluck its bloom
then walk the depths of green-wood and young fawn
scampers deftly to early morning's song,
the dew, collected by each web, hangs silk
as love unrequited steels from the wrong
moments of the day and pearl night time's milk.
There dwelt within my heart, one harp—pristine
the upland music of its gaze divine,
and hour by hour it lent its plucked lament
to all who hear within the soul, repent.
The flow'r forever, sorrowful and just,
reaps bounty in the music as it must.

Sea sanded the shore like a piece of wood
and it became smooth as liquid silver,
loving to the earth and sky, salty, cold—
the end destiny of every river;
and I stood with my back to the forest
watching the sun's last fading purple light,
the once burgeoning moon, rising poorest
from a refugee camp in desert night,
where the fire is the only comfort, red
as a mind contorted by the black fear
of having naught, and the distance now said
to be a symbol of indifference near
death, and refusing to dream the future,
which now takes hands and is stately sutured.

The light to bear at my last humble breath,
the goblet of oil, cast out purest gold,
all speak of favour's now placed laurel wreath—
the best reward when I am creased and old.
I shall with folded hands, resting, here pray
for my heart's desire to not be lost when
I am gone, the print words to stop saying
all that was delicate and austere then.
For I am but a savage beast, beauty
in my time that cloaked a sorry pink smile
(that chapstick almost choked with song's glory),
in hunter's boots, and brought the deer from miles.
Ne'er in my lifetime did I leave for good,
I always would return with one proved poem.

The flock of geese landed before nightfall,
the sword of beauty divided night's flight—
the crimson breath of sunset's remnant might
repeated in the pond's caressing tall
shadows growing wide and with the moon's white
arm overhead, a clear, smooth, pensive gloss,
reflection on the water, strung with moss,
was riveting and studied, grey and bright—
the two facets submerging 'neath waters
pure, dark night's last star on the horizon:
echoing each other's fascination
and morbid still dance, where nature gathers.
The pondering of creature's dust to dust,
and speaking of the life to morning's crust.

In every just endeavor, let there be
the peal of every heartbeat's thunder loud,
creed from minds of persuasion's honour cloud,
harbinger of happenstance destiny.
In every long-studied word let there be
nourishment to the veins of auburn earth,
great victory, and discourse to unearth,
a veritable map to cross each sea.
In every precious new dream let there be
a moment where it started as a seed,
germinating from a small sterling bead,
and the dawning moment we could all see.
What started as illusion made its choice
to subdue you as its servant in voice.

When turns the weather to a fierce grey storm,
we plunge into the cover of the trees,
we reign in all our damp with leaf-light's keys,
we take a liking to our thrift dry form,
and for clothing, branches spar decorum,
while flowers decorate the hair, and bees
dance smitten o'er the green treacherously,
now creatures of the woodland and the morn—
we once wore dress within the looking glass
and talked in shadows of the evening's lace;
the sun-filled hours were traipsing to the dance
in diametric meter of the class,
we spun to charity of solemn face,
and bowed to light, enamoured in this spance.

A Rose From Thorns

A bud emerged in snowy steeple-white,
clear as champagne was the high-bred morning,
the night reeled back, deliciously warming
the gossamer threads of a spider's might.
A rose grew in dewy stained-glass temple
from sharp thorns that pierced a Saviour's pure brow,
and the garden was wildness constrained now,
cultivated flow'r to mind the simple.
Our lives were complex without the bouquet,
so we plucked each sweetly stained soul of rose,
and the summer wafted innocent prose,
nuances of physician's tourniquet.
If only love would heal the fevered mind,
but oil from roses soothes the heart in kind.

We parted with one last embrace and I
stood alone against the world—one small dove—
earth had abandoned me like a lost love,
then I flew upwards into a red sky.
I landed far away on Railway Trail,
and covered my neck in a small alcove,
beautiful as the sunshine resin rove,
streaming, ever streaming, tempering failed
heart from despair to hope and faith—like rings
I wear to ward off the dark in this time.
My sturdiness is now a gift in rain,
and climbing the ancient mountain I sing,
walking toward the curse of the weather's nine
furious storms, pitted against the grain.

Section II: The Victoriana Sonnets

hills ache with silence where their hymns would ring
as a bell breaks solitude, mutiny.

—Emily Isaacson

Jacob's Ladder

Early in the morn, wee lassie, our sun
belongs only to us, as to new day:
the trees move on the cliffs with the wind, run—
gallop as the livery of thoughts stray.
There's a fair space where we spoke in burnished
freedom to tell the ancient firelight tales,
behold the minds of youth were once furnished
with reason and rhyme, cloaked with silver mail
of the righteous who walk to church to sing.
Now they've forgotten the song of the tree,
hills ache with silence where their hymns would ring
as a bell breaks solitude, mutiny.
Taxed, they will climb until they climb no more;
the Ladder of Jacob fell to the poor.

Salty Purse

That one low call of evening, stuttered breath,
arrested my thought and dragged it away:
more than moving rain symphonies in May,
wildflowers for the heads of women, wreathed,
children who would never tire and grow old
playing forever in the dusty street,
golden heads in a field of hard red wheat,
shivering by a heater in the cold,
reciting civil lines of English verse,
then hoping for the conscience's token piece,
but subsisting on the fare of crabmeat,
remnant of the blue ocean's salty purse.
Whatever we may tire of while the poor,
is now the indulgence of those with more.

Vintage Lamp

Observing a vintage lampshade in hand,
questioning the blue shadows and the light
that serenades the infant born in bright
starched fabric crib, the blurry tempest land—
the servant stands, beating the cooling palm.
The sculpture of the lamp's enamelled base,
athlete of all pertaining to the race
toward morning—the resistance's oily balm,
mother of this era, a busy throng
moving on, smoky denouement in form
telling of the path beneath my feet worn
to candles from the lamp of moonlit song.
Grassroots binding of the look from wasteful
to the cry for ancient things more tasteful.

Spikenard Madonna

When you stood in the brightened dawn of youth,
morning sun lit your head to searing flame,
the jewel that was your crown bore your name,
and scepter bent authority to truth.
We were orphans, standing in your courtyard,
no bliss of parenthood to claim our fate,
no blimey kiss of death to stir our hate,
she took a bottle of ancient spikenard.
Madonna bore us, pouring out her oil;
she called us all her child in heart matters,
our minds, in retrospect, once wore tatters.
In gingham aprons we would cook and toil,
in the woods and fields, our hands would quick spy
what nature left, rust berries for the pie.

Cherry Trees in Blossom

Where the cherry trees touch dusk in descant—
wine branches blossom effulgent bright white,
all darkness of the time for this full night—
I wander 'neath the fading light, recant.
Seasons of my soul were like a grand home
I sojourned in once, for the staid calling
when all life pauses before the falling.
The invalid was destined to find none
of the aforementioned illness beneath
these eaves of healthy grandeur, sunlight near
the slant of shadows, refracted prism tear
that moved over the house, the sea, the heath.
If I, in fury, could my earth restrain,
I would—a hundred blossoms in my train.

Section III: The Hallmark Sonnets

My artisan bread contains the berries
and the last cream rose petals from the arch
over the garden's entrance in the park . . .

—Emily Isaacson

Remember me, though friendless now I be,
when through the parting sash I waved so cold,
and when the downpour drenched me growing old,
it was your friendship I desired to see.
Your chestnut hair was like the autumn's end,
then parted as a river from its source,
your red lips spoke in snows like holly boughs—
poisonous green, yet comely to defend.
My eyes have now been opened, I was fair
to every friend I valued in the mirror,
my foes live in a realistic fear
I'd intuit my neighbours and their cares.
If only I'd extend my hands in grace,
I'd look upon a multicultural face.

The light shone out a little bleary-eyed,
from every casement window to the night,
it was the little house that glimmered bright,
we walked the lake road to the water's side.
It was the home that we had waited for,
it spoke to us of hearth and firelight,
the attic rooms kept children within sight,
the plans we had would make us long for more.
Beneath the eaves the memories were dear,
and countless others had this way come by,
with dreams romantic, lovers that would tie
their hearts unto each other, ever near.
We counted every penny with intent,
but came up short, with modest discontent.

When I have lived my years, I shall recall
of days when I would not recant my youth,
the hours I walked among the sandy dunes,
observing gulls that flew 'till they were small
upon horizons far 'neath dusty moon.
My mother was the sea, my father, sun—
I was the morning light through seaweed dun,
that tides had strung the shore we walked so soon.
If anything in childhood I regret,
my life would be too sentimental now,
when auburn frames an alabaster brow,
the names of all my starfish I'd forget.
What word I spoke in child-like melody,
became the verse that echoed from the sea.

Ode to Canada

My country was the destination near—
of immigrant, traveller, visitors,
and men and women sojourned on our shore—
made haste from old dominions rung with tears—
They left in boats as Syrian refugees,
the dead of night had hid them, and they rowed,
arriving with their children in the flow
of time, through oceans, poverty's disease.
To freedom!—people called with libertine.
Their hearts were softened to a native land
where people stood together hand in hand.
Their eyes were opened, they began to sing—
We are the patriot wanderers home,
in all of us command our hearts aglow!

There was a light that burned upon the prow,
the figure of a woman in its mast,
in dark, the isle of drudgery was passed,
and ram-rod straight she stood with salted brow.
The moon reflected on her seeing eyes
that looked into the distance with constraint
the figurehead of politics restrained,
she was not fearful of their dreadful lies.
Unyielding at the storm of every task,
she sailed as ship 'Restorer' through each sea,
her silvered hair of wood hailed ocean's lea,
the water lilies bowed for living last,
forgotten, starboard's view of fading light:
today has gone, tomorrow will arise.

The city bourgeoned by the waterside,
an isle of apple blossom, steady pink,
and winter skated sorrow 'round the rink.
Through former age, in word and deed, now bide,
to resolution, cavalier and bold,
that evil will not fall upon the mild,
and vales of lilies grow 'till they are wild.
We picked fiery bouquets, as we were cold,
and mothers gathered families 'round the vase,
and walkers of the road were doubly blessed,
by nature's bounty, giv'n at their request,
a boy who heard the gilded ringing paused.
For history was reticent and kind
at island's song repeating on the mind.

When I would give my parting glance to thee,
when I would bid thee my austere good bye—
I give you my respect with lowered eyes—
passing by you, I would imagine me
with you, a better heaven than before.
I saw you rise to glory without qualm,
the storms of life had all resolved to calm.
Your aging rage had crashed upon the shore
as you conceded life was not to be
forever and forever of thy breath,
but families continue on into the next
years, and generations rise to thank thee.
When I would pay my last respects, in laud,
we all would give your well-deserved applause.

City of flowers, sweet moments at will,
remember me lonely as a kindness,
a sea-sick isle swept with reminiscence,
from starry wood-fenced meadow to the hill.
I played beneath the poplar trees at school,
a delicate child with gold braided hair:
I was your poet, knelt, composing there,
pupil of the largest transcendent pool.
Your children, Thetis and Saltspring, come by
for tea in a garden of fine incense,
steaming rose hips and lingering reasons
for conversing with a true butterfly:
sending you their translucent wing letters,
setting your thoughts free from iron fetters.

Lovely, my lovely when the night has passed,
I dream, though waking, my tears on your face,
I have lived my lifetime, and now your grace
has wakened me once more to autumn's last:
the leaves all turning as a crimson tide
vacating Dallas Point becomes the fall,
the moments before winter's silent call,
and the last mother stone cathedral's chide.
Her bells have rung out in the Sunday morn,
the whitened light through stained glass, glowing peers,
and falling snow will wait 'till late next year,
'till after the new dairy calves are born.
Fortuitous that I have heard you call,
before the ground is frozen, shadows tall.

Soldier-like, bravest man a rising moon—
backs to earth—there is a war—they'd open
their eyes, if on their eyes they could depend,
before all loyal sons lie in their tombs.
Hills, look to the hills—who'll join me, not one?
No longer have I a friend to think of,
all my patriot friends are fallen doves.
No one thinks better than of his own son,
a mother's tear would not forget this morn—
for here I stand, a lonely soldier last.
Fly from me enemy! Fly from my past!
I have courage for war until I'm torn,
and it is fully time, fly from me then.
Undeceive thyself from my contagion.

The Freeman

Now to the world that has put me in chains,
I will laugh again, beyond this oak tree,
for I was once driven too, to be free—
there lies another prison when it rains:
there lies another logic that compels,
when forced to plant a marigold, plant ten,
throw seeds into the ground beyond land's bend,
my father, in the harvest time it tells
you were on a ladder of broken rungs,
chores burden you when you are ancient now,
with all the winds that have passed through your boughs.
You helped right the fallen trees, roped their trunks
so now they're back to back in allegiance;
no longer fallen, in a freedom stance.

A voice cries out, I dare not turn my head,
the abyss is deep and to its depths I see
it red with flame or blood! Turn away thee,
fatal path, woe to those who want me dead.
I shall not touch the wound that gored so deep:
not faithful love—the duty of a wife,
she's fortunate without their passion's strife.
Incumbents of religion now would weep,
if no one would oppose mental cruelty;
for this has been a battered, silent church,
not one voice uttered not one febrile word,
to encourage some brutal brass fealty.
There is always tomorrow to resolve
the hearts of our dear marriages dissolved.

The horses, stirred up, in the darkening France,
went thundering down the hill every which way,
I hid in terror from their highland neigh,
behind a trunk, while holding to a branch.
It was magnolias upon the tree,
their fragrance was as gospel to my heart,
rivalling holy scriptures from the start,
the gardener had planted much for me.
Without regret, I knew that I was saved
from illiterate end without a book—
for I was cloaked in words, ink shod my foot,
without debt, in the black, I calmly stayed.
For writing is divine when free from fear;
reflection's more successful in the mirror.

If ever you were mine, don't leave me pearls,
my eyes brim with tears at your advancing
years, your leopard prints and tango dancing
into the looking glass with whitening curls.
You once were very beautiful and sweet,
the men that took your picture held their heads,
they courted with intentions you were wed,
they benefitted you with Purdy's treats—
How momentary is a compliment
unless a woman's character is built,
a castle on the sand is anchored silt—
foundation of a home is wet cement.
Oh now, my darling, do not look at me,
for I am beautiful, but never seen.

When I started at this one quarter note,
perfect order of a five finger scale,
it became something of a killer whale
by Beethoven, black and white emotive
played for background noise called the Für Elise.
My classical training at dawn each day
never let me forget my practice way—
my gilded lily was a fleur-de-lis.
For I was only small and a witness—
you are my father and you put my first
coat on my back before we went to church,
my brief spoken prayers were the crucifix—
beyond religion to the spirituals—
lend me your depth, I practice rituals.

If you have loved me, I have not complied,
although I dance with you to our first tune,
float by on the canals beneath the moon,
the oar for this gondola you supplied.
The yellow coat I thoughtfully recall,
I hung my reverie on your door hook,
I remembered hungrily every book
you recommend, every word read, the small
bowed tell-tale things of yours I don't forget:
your leather briefcase, your love of dark
coffee, Turkish tea that started it all—
the contest of wills to see who was met
by strangers in foreign lands and who stayed
home. But we both had degrees of straying.

A Handful of Blackberries

The last of light has faded with the night,
and shadows disappear into the dark,
the sun is now forgotten like last lark,
and rounded moon is captive to this light.
Walking with a handful of blackberries,
I'm nestled deep inside my guarded stance,
I'm made of stone, unblinking in a trance,
I wrestled with the thorn bush then tarried.
My artisan bread contains the berries
and the last cream rose petals from the arch
over the garden's entrance in the park
there, where my truest friend was once married.
We walked on friendship's path of watermere,
and contemplated future moments dear.

I am an agent blind of all sadness,
I am deaf of mournful mysteries! Still
of misery made from a cup of chilled
white wine—one dime, recalled work in darkness.
Soul, I cannot tell. I am urged to run
by impetuous breath and false decree;
I fall and fall in swift descent to thee.
I am at the bottom of a well, done,
better if I pull myself up by my
bootstraps and go down to the potter's brown
stone house. If sometimes, I dare turn and frown,
it is that I have never met the sky:
pots and works of clay that were amber red.
Potter with so much coloured glaze, my head!

The clock chimes eight, and through the window pane,
the light so dim, my dear, at evening's end,
and purposefully twilight bows its head;
it never poured anointing on the lane,
but walking to this antique house you came,
with walking stick beside you striking stone,
and rivulets of water ran alone,
across the cobbled pathway just the same.
You saw me through an uncorrupted lens,
I was an age-old book you'd read before,
from the glass teapot, wintermint was poured,
we spoke in lowered tones at time's expense,
before the cherished crystal breaks and cries,
a boreal reflection of the skies.

Your last word in this pallid hospice realm
was miniscule as round millet is small,
impossible to catch beyond the hall,
yet indicative of golden ship's helm,
voyage looming onward into heaven,
far beyond this one sombre meaning filled
room, fragrant with flowers on the white sill,
from each child beneath your heart, all seven.
In righteous clothing you are finely dressed,
there was a call to you once with meaning,
past the world's inebriated dreaming;
what word of praise to give the very blessed?
The last moment with you I saw a door
you opened to the sick, the homeless, poor.

Go catch a mouse in your medieval life,
for Persian cats these days have not changed tin
to bronze; I would that you go out, yet in
you come, no alchemist of human strife.
You chased a dandelion's last feather,
and watched the drooping rose lay down its head,
you curled up in a cozy basket bed,
your down was damp from terrible weather.
What'ere I wish, it likely will not be,
and I could cross my fingers, hope to spy,
while serving chlorophyll in salmon pie,
around a cat as difficult as me.
With luck, she never actually offends,
she utters loud meows with no pretense.

Many red apples of your orchard grow,
each rust variety I could desire,
eaten fresh or roasted over the fire,
glow in deep burgundy, magenta, rose.
You harvest the supernatural book,
to feed a town not far from the river,
from the King James' version, reading scripture—
an Abbott was once fording the clear brook.
They sold your ripe fruit at the marketplace,
McIntosh, Spartans, piled high in wood bins—
you were a ruffian, who's forgiven,
you offered help to the lady with lace,
she crocheted doilies for your table,
where the fruit bowl would sit and be stable.

If I am set in my maturing ways,
I may be now an octave not a note,
lest drawing years now catch me by the throat,
and victimless the world would seldom stay,
held dear, a crime of passionless embrace.
The echoes of the weapon on my neck,
the tumbling fingers keeping me in check,
the slant upon my skin of scar's necklace.
I would be still a frightened Northern star,
now gleaming through each variegated tree,
aurora borealis glowed briefly
if I was to imagine life unmarred.
You sent me sterling, my lover was new,
I was to sail in a cedar canoe.

When you retreat alone into the wood,
you are familiar with places forlorn,
you bow your silver horn, a unicorn,
and the poetic verse is now your food.
Look into the bright spiritual domain,
and see if heaven's walls are high and close,
see if the door is open thee or closed,
look to the tower, the castle maintained
an archer, with a rainbow, sky to sky,
seek in thine arsenal the armour shined
for all of sixty years—thou art still mine,
beneath all sorrows that the poor would spy,
for we are never cruel nor cold, betrothed,
our hearts glow with our kindness and our love.

Beside the red warmth of your roaring hearth,
I draw myself up to your friends' circle
and the firelight dims to blue and purple,
the flickering stories revealed your mirth.
On the avenue of constellations
I walk upon the stars on the pavement,
everyone has a name in the cement,
their gold street of stellar revelations.
There is a home in your soul of contrasts:
I find a virtue in your caverns dark
that shines, a vein of gold within a lark,
some streak of light made you lonely grasses,
where the wild birds would swoop and make their nests
here the poorest peasants make their homes best.

When you are near to the tiny new babe,
extravagant love in coming to earth,
the incarnation of his virgin birth,
the light of the gospel that will not fade . . .
Listen to the reason for his kindness
to us: the season of rejoicing tells
of gifts from the Magi, frankincense smells
of beauty, myrrh restores our innocence.
Gold is the enduring royalty now,
an immediacy with God's future—
our lives are now restored to us, sutured,
and sin is no longer the altar bowed.
To the underworld, death! For Christ is born—
if he should then die with bright crown of thorns.

There are black figs that grow from thistle's brier,
pears ripen from ev'ry Calvary's thorn,
there is a land called heav'n—it is the morn—
and it descends on us within our mire.
My pristine view could spy its pearlesque gate,
from place of inky darkness I would look
from page to page inside an aging book,
the twelve tall oaken wall clocks growing late.
We don't aspire as children to be short,
nor looked upon with unrealistic eyes,
nor told our Saviour bleeds for us and cries,
not when the adults do console with port.
I thought I'd leave some burgundy for you,
or seltzer water with a lime ice cube.

Now to my end I come in stately black,
for I am but a prisoner of this earth,
I can't escape its clutches or its wrath,
nor any of its loves, nor laughs, nor births.
I bear the lovely France a final fleur,
I witness of this hour before the flame,
for all my visions have been of one cœur—
I cry to God, unyielding of his name.
Do not my hands untie, lest I recant—
for I am but a bird that cannot fly.
Do not relent, for I shall not repent;
my sweetest fame is written now on high.
You look upon my pure and martyred face,
that in the flame of love has found its grace.

If I have loved you in a thousand ways,
I have lit a thousand candles for you.
I have made a fire and cooked a beef stew.
My heart is sincere, my mind never strays:
I would but give a thousand gifts that morn,
if my life held you in one thousand wings,
if I gave away a half-dozen things,
my sentimental songs you would not scorn.
One thousand carollers stood at your door,
there was no unserved guest, no unmet need
before your home of hospitality,
and each one ringing louder than before.
I'll laugh again before my life is through,
because you have loved me and I've loved you.

O flame that circles me—O wisdom's light,
seeking the way through my utter darkness,
hurtling from the outside through the starkness
to the inside of my heart, a dark night
of the soul cannot distance purer thee—
for I would write in ink your mind untold,
and fashion you as from clay to the world,
until the blind could endless, boundless see.
Through obsession I would find my novice;
she would be of one love and one desire,
lone in a convent cell she would retire.
She is blessed olive without one vice,
of a still-chaste, and contemplative place—
now humans could not boast to see this face.

Section IV: The Apothecary's Daughter Sonnets

I have many flowers in my garden,
each smells so sweetly of the summer's air,
envelopes of colour, secret wardens . . .

—Emily Isaacson

Do not despise thou love, nor rue its share,
the shelter it provides is providence,
the elegance of home is free from cares,
and thine bent head in prayer is evidence.
I have many flowers in my garden,
each smells so sweetly of the summer's air,
envelopes of colour, secret wardens,
for all the trust that heav'n keeps guarded there.
If ever I should give my heart to one,
I would find her 'neath an arbour waiting;
my intimations second to her none,
there'd be one song in my mouth abating:
I would give thee my youth's flattery now
that I may not prove false upon thy vow.

Last was I to read your cream folded note,
when I was still quite young, I would not laugh
at your sincerity, and my wood staff.
My reputation was my ivory throat.
I would take you at your word, upon sea
I float: saline is my buffer, salt pure
that reaches deep into my wounds, censured
as crystalline mine salt, deep in the green,
we move, we float, licensed liquidity.
And now the years have almost passed me by,
I remember you, the boy that once kythed
in books and music, gardens' flow'r to me.
Do not let me forget the passing age,
that once held me, a player, on the stage.

Section V: The Highway of Tears

Yet, one car stopped and would not pass me by,
he motioned too, with ulterior name,
then signalled me, a moth unto his flame . . .

—Emily Isaacson

Sonnet of Tears

Along the Highway of Tears, far from home,
I was deep in my own heart as I hummed,
the cars in multicoloured rhythm drummed
a stretch of road so lonely I could roam.
Yet, one car stopped and would not pass me by,
he motioned too, with ulterior name,
then signalled me, a moth unto his flame,
avoiding the dark rain, I sat inside.
As sea birds fly into the bulwark's brine
waters, cresting ocean, I was caught up
by the notion I was saved—and by love,
we struggled at the next stop 'neath the pines.
A silenced mind, I was no longer free,
beaten, my heart, was resting on his knees.